FRANCIS FRITH'S

# WARWICKSHIRE
## REVISITED

### PHOTOGRAPHIC MEMORIES

**JULIE ROYLE** was born in Cheshire and grew up there and in Northumbria. She studied history at the University of Exeter because she wanted to live in the West Country. She now lives near Worcester, in a small country cottage with a large unruly garden, and works as a freelance photographer and writer specialising in landscape, wildlife, travel, conservation, environmental issues and local history. She has a passion for Africa, which she has visited many times, but loves Britain too, particularly the English Lake District.

FRANCIS FRITH'S
PHOTOGRAPHIC MEMORIES

# WARWICKSHIRE
## REVISITED

### PHOTOGRAPHIC MEMORIES

JULIE ROYLE

First published in hardback in the United Kingdom in 2006 by
The Francis Frith Collection®

Hardback Edition 2006
ISBN 1-85937-652-5

British Library Cataloguing in Publication Data

Warwickshire Revisited Photographic Memories
Julie Royle
ISBN 1-85937-652-5

The Francis Frith Collection®
Frith's Barn, Teffont,
Salisbury, Wiltshire SP3 5QP
Tel: +44 (0) 1722 716 376
Email: info@francisfrith.co.uk
www.francisfrith.com

Printed and bound in Great Britain

Front Cover: **WARWICK**, *High Street 1922* 72343t
Frontispiece: **WARWICK**, *East Gate 1922* 72349

*The colour-tinting is for illustrative purposes only, and is not intended
to be historically accurate*

# CONTENTS

# FRANCIS FRITH
## VICTORIAN PIONEER

FRANCIS FRITH, founder of the world-famous photographic archive, was a complex and multi-talented man. A devout Quaker and a highly successful Victorian businessman, he was philosophical by nature and pioneering in outlook.

By 1855 he had already established a wholesale grocery business in Liverpool, and sold it for the astonishing sum of £200,000, which is the equivalent today of over £15,000,000. Now a very rich man, he was able to indulge his passion for travel. As a child he had pored over travel books written by early explorers, and his fancy and imagination had been stirred by family holidays to the sublime mountain regions of Wales and Scotland. 'What lands of spirit-stirring and enriching scenes and places!' he had written. He was to return to these scenes of grandeur in later years to 'recapture the thousands of vivid and tender memories', but with a different purpose. Now in his thirties, and captivated by the new science of photography, Frith set out on a series of pioneering journeys up the Nile and

to the Near East that occupied him from 1856 until 1860.

### INTRIGUE AND EXPLORATION

These far-flung journeys were packed with intrigue and adventure. In his life story, written when he was sixty-three, Frith tells of being held captive by bandits, and of fighting 'an awful midnight battle to the very point of surrender with a deadly pack of hungry, wild dogs'. Wearing flowing Arab costume, Frith arrived at Akaba by camel sixty years before Lawrence of Arabia, where he encountered 'desert princes and rival sheikhs, blazing with jewel-hilted swords'.

He was the first photographer to venture beyond the sixth cataract of the Nile. Africa was still the mysterious 'Dark Continent', and Stanley and Livingstone's historic meeting was a decade into the future. The conditions for picture taking confound belief. He laboured for hours in his wicker dark-room in the sweltering heat of the desert, while the volatile chemicals fizzed dangerously in their trays. Back in London he exhibited his photographs and was 'rapturously cheered' by members of the Royal Society. His reputation as a photographer was made overnight.

### VENTURE OF A LIFE-TIME

Characteristically, Frith quickly spotted the opportunity to create a new business as a specialist publisher of photographs. He lived in an era of immense and sometimes violent change.

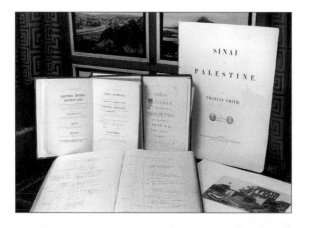

For the poor in the early part of Victoria's reign work was exhausting and the hours long, and people had precious little free time to enjoy themselves. Most had no transport other than a cart or gig at their disposal, and rarely travelled far beyond the boundaries of their own town or village. However, by the 1870s the railways had threaded their way across the country, and Bank Holidays and half-day Saturdays had been made obligatory by Act of Parliament. All of a sudden the working man and his family were able to enjoy days out and see a little more of the world.

With typical business acumen, Francis Frith foresaw that these new tourists would enjoy having souvenirs to commemorate their days out. In 1860 he married Mary Ann Rosling and set out on a new career: his aim was to photograph every city, town and village in Britain. For the next thirty years he travelled the country by train and by pony and trap, producing fine photographs of seaside resorts and beauty spots that were keenly bought by millions of Victorians. These prints were painstakingly pasted into family albums and pored over during the dark nights of winter, rekindling precious memories of summer excursions.

## THE RISE OF FRITH & CO

Frith's studio was soon supplying retail shops all over the country. To meet the demand he gathered about him a small team of photographers, and published the work of independent artist-photographers of the calibre of Roger Fenton and Francis Bedford. In order to gain some understanding of the scale of Frith's business one only has to look at the catalogue issued by Frith & Co in 1886: it runs to some 670 pages, listing not only many thousands of views of the British Isles but also many photographs of most European countries, and China, Japan, the USA and Canada - note the sample page shown on page 9 from the hand-written Frith & Co ledgers recording the pictures. By 1890 Frith had created the greatest specialist photographic publishing company in the world, with over 2,000 sales outlets - more than the combined number that Boots and WH Smith have today! The picture on the next page shows the Frith & Co display board at Ingleton in the Yorkshire Dales (left of window). Beautifully constructed with a mahogany frame and gilt inserts, it could display up to a dozen local scenes.

## POSTCARD BONANZA

The ever-popular holiday postcard we know today took many years to develop. In 1870 the Post Office issued the first plain cards, with a pre-printed stamp on one face. In 1894 they allowed other publishers' cards to be sent through the mail with an attached adhesive halfpenny stamp. Demand grew rapidly, and in 1895 a new size of postcard was permitted called the court card, but there was little room for illustration. In 1899, a year after Frith's death, a new card measuring 5.5 x 3.5 inches became the standard format, but it was not until 1902 that the divided back came into being, so that the address and message could be on one face and a full-size illustration on the other. Frith & Co were in the vanguard of postcard development: Frith's sons Eustace and Cyril continued their father's monumental task, expanding the number of views offered to the public and recording more and more places in Britain, as the coasts and countryside were opened up to mass travel.

Francis Frith had died in 1898 at his villa in Cannes, his great project still growing. The archive he created continued in business for another seventy years. By 1970 it contained over a third of a million pictures showing 7,000 British towns and villages.

## FRANCIS FRITH'S LEGACY

Frith's legacy to us today is of immense significance and value, for the magnificent archive of evocative photographs he created provides a unique record of change in the cities, towns and villages throughout Britain over a century and more. Frith and his fellow studio photographers revisited locations many times down the years to update their views, compiling for us an enthralling and colourful pageant of British life and character.

We are fortunate that Frith was dedicated to recording the minutiae of everyday life. For it is this sheer wealth of visual data, the painstaking chronicle of changes in dress, transport, street layouts, buildings, housing, engineering and landscape that captivates us so much today. His remarkable images offer us a powerful link with the past and with the lives of our ancestors.

## THE VALUE OF THE ARCHIVE TODAY

Computers have now made it possible for Frith's many thousands of images to be accessed almost instantly. Frith's images are increasingly used as visual resources, by social historians, by researchers into genealogy and ancestry, by architects and town planners, and by teachers involved in local history projects.

In addition, the archive offers every one of us an opportunity to examine the places where we and our families have lived and worked down the years. Highly successful in Frith's own era, the archive is now, a century and more on, entering a new phase of popularity. Historians consider the Francis Frith Collection to be of prime national importance. It is the only archive of its kind remaining in private ownership. Francis Frith's archive is now housed in an historic timber barn in the beautiful village of Teffont in Wiltshire. Its founder would not recognize the archive office as it is today. In place of the many thousands of dusty boxes containing glass plate negatives and an all-pervading odour of photographic chemicals, there are now ranks of computer screens. He would be amazed to watch his images travelling round the world at unimaginable speeds through internet lines.

The archive's future is both bright and exciting. Francis Frith, with his unshakeable belief in making photographs available to the greatest number of people, would undoubtedly approve of what is being done today with his lifetime's work. His photographs depicting our shared past are now bringing pleasure and enlightenment to millions around the world a century and more after his death.

# WARWICKSHIRE REVISITED
## AN INTRODUCTION

WARWICKSHIRE has traditionally been called 'the heart of England', and geographically that is exactly what it is, being about as far from the sea as one can get, and surrounded by seven other landlocked counties. But 'heart of England' is not just a geographical term; it is also a symbolic one. It represents a romantic ideal of Englishness itself, made manifest in a rural patchwork of rolling farmland, woodland and hedgerows, dissected by willow-fringed rivers meandering dreamily through flower-filled meadows. Scattered throughout this imagined idyll are charming villages, each with thatch-roofed, rose-draped cottages nestling beside an old stone church and a welcoming timber-framed pub where a fire roars forever in the grate and fruit machines will never gain a foothold.

It is not like that any more, but there are a few places where one can almost believe it is. What *is* true is that Warwickshire is predominantly rural, and has been since the Local Government Act of 1974 stripped Birmingham, Solihull and

**NUNEATON,** *Queen's Road c1945* N89017

10

Coventry from the county. That still left it with a fair number of towns, but none of them is of any great size, though Leamington, Nuneaton and Rugby do seem to be expanding at the speed of light. There are several small and medium-sized market towns: places such as Alcester, Henley-in-Arden, Shipston-on-Stour, Stratford-upon-Avon and Warwick, whose centres retain considerable charm, even as their characterless suburbs penetrate ever deeper into the countryside. Overall, however, Warwickshire is a county of villages, though they are not what they once were. In the typical village, ancient cottages are dwarfed by extensions and blighted by uPVC or dark-stained timber window frames. Roofs and walls sprout TV aerials, satellite dishes and burglar alarms, gardens are hedged with suburban leylandii and people-carriers are crammed onto every driveway. House names such as The Old Schoolhouse, The Old Post Office, The Old Smithy and The Old Stores tell us all we need to know about village amenities. Bus services are reduced, the church is kept locked most of the time, and the pub is only just clinging on to life. And yet, the more services shrink, the more the villages grow. New developments surround the old cottages, but the styles and materials employed owe nothing to the local vernacular. Garish, car-related signage proliferates, and roads are subject to 'traffic-calming' measures which would be ugly even when applied in an urban setting, but monstrous in formerly attractive rural lanes. Some villages do remain relatively unspoilt, but not many. The Warwickshire so beautifully illustrated in this book is getting harder to find.

Traditionally, Warwickshire was divided into two: Feldon and Arden. The Feldon, south of the River Avon, was famed nationwide for its prosperous farms, which combined pasture and arable, and for its charming villages, many of them with impressive 'wool churches' built with the wealth generated by the sheep. North of the Avon, the Forest of Arden is hillier, with poorer soil, less of it under the plough, much of it wooded in times past. Shakespeare's *As You Like It* was set in Arden, and around Henley and Tanworth there are places where the landscape is still recognisably that of the Arden he knew: a pleasing mix of pasture, hedges, copses and ponds. What he would not recognise is the roar of the M40 and M42.

Warwickshire has no dramatic natural features. The Avon, despite its fame, is essentially a modest little river. There are no hills of any size, but that is not to say that the county is entirely flat. Much of it undulates pleasantly; and the south, where Warwickshire has a small share of the Cotswolds, is almost hilly in a very gentle sort of way. The highest point is Ilmington Down, on the Gloucestershire border, which reaches a modest 850ft. Edge Hill, and its beautifully named neighbour, Sun Rising Hill, form a noticeable escarpment. The formerly delightful Burton Dassett Hills have been blighted by the M40.

Warwickshire is second only to London in the number of foreign visitors it attracts. They do not come for the scenery: it is the literary and historical associations that bring them. Shakespeare is the main draw, but Warwickshire is incredibly rich in history and in what the tourism industry likes to call 'heritage'. There is not much in the way of early history: prehistoric people left only a small imprint on Warwickshire, and so did the Romans, though Watling Street, Ryknild

Street and the Fosse Way all pass through the county. After the Romans withdrew, successive waves of Anglo-Saxon invaders began to arrive. It was they who began large-scale forest clearance for agriculture, created the shire system and founded so many of the towns and villages which form the basis of modern Warwickshire. The county was part of Mercia, one of the most dynamic of Anglo-Saxon kingdoms. Its most notable king was Offa, who ruled from 757 to 796 and for whom the village of Offchurch, near Leamington, is named. It was during Offa's reign that Warwick was founded, but it was destroyed by Danish invaders and had to be re-founded and re-fortified in about 915 by King Alfred's daughter Ethelfleda, known as the Lady of the Mercians.

The arrival of the Normans in the late 11th century brought great changes to Warwickshire. They believed in establishing political, military and psychological dominance by building powerful castles to overawe potential enemies. The mighty fortresses at Warwick and Kenilworth were established at this time. For the next 500 years or more these two castles, along with the county in general, were to be associated with some of the greatest (and most notorious) names and events in English history: Henry II, King John, Richard Neville (Warwick the Kingmaker), John of Gaunt, Simon de Montfort (Father of the English Parliament), Henry VIII, Elizabeth I, Robert Dudley, Charles I, Oliver Cromwell, the Barons' War, the Wars of the Roses, the English Civil War, the Gunpowder Plot, to name but a few. Shakespeare recorded episodes from Warwickshire's history in his plays, and Sir Walter Scott celebrated the glories of Kenilworth in his eponymous novel. Scott also, incidentally, believed the view of Warwick Castle towering over the River Avon to be 'unsurpassed' in all England. Several other places in the county attract similar verdicts: Compton Wynyates, for example, is believed by many to be the most beautiful country house in England. In fact, Warwickshire has numerous country houses and 'stately homes' of the very highest

**STRATFORD UPON AVON,** *The River Avon 1922* 72395

quality, including Baddesley Clinton, Upton House, Farnborough Hall, Coughton Court and Packwood House.

Modern times have not been kind to Warwickshire. With Birmingham and Coventry detached from the county it has relatively little from the days of the Industrial Revolution, but 20th-century industry has left its mark in the north, where coal was mined for a time. Kingsbury, for instance, was a mining town and still bears the scars. On top of that, it has been lumbered with oil storage depots, industrial estates, waste disposal sites, major roads and a motorway. Or consider the tragedy of Nuneaton, another coalfield town, which was packed with Victorian buildings of immense character, but lost most of them in the second half of the 20th century, when they were demolished to make way for a dreadful ring road and a collection of modern buildings of almost unimaginable horribleness. Even Stratford has its share of disasters. It is hard to imagine how the modern buildings near the church could possibly have been considered appropriate, and there are some hideous structures on the main shopping streets. Fortunately, it is only a scattering, and the overall impression remains favourable - but why was it allowed to happen, here of all places? And even Warwick, beautiful Warwick, does not survive unscathed - what a shock it is to the first-time visitor to be suddenly confronted with the sheer mind-blowing awfulness of the council offices and public library. How could they do that to Warwick?

The real disaster, however, is that Warwickshire has become what a newspaper once described as 'the motorway hub of England' - and that was in the 1970s, when the worst was still to come. The M6, the M40, the M42, the M45 and the M69 all pass through Warwickshire, and the M1 skirts it, adding its own noise and fumes to the rest. Of all these, the M40 is the most heart-breaking for those who loved Warwickshire as it was. It is impossible to overstate the damage done by this motorway, which slices mercilessly through what was the loveliest countryside in the county. Today, there is nowhere in Warwickshire where the sound of traffic cannot be heard.

**LEAMINGTON SPA,** *The Railway Bridge 1892* 30986

# WARWICK, LEAMINGTON AND KENILWORTH

**WARWICK,** *The Castle from the River 1892*
30997

Warwick Castle is one of the most impressive buildings in the country, and constitutes one of England's classic views when seen from Castle Bridge; a view which is at its best when the trees are in full leaf, masking the houses at Bridge End whose gardens sweep down to the south bank of the Avon.

**WARWICK**
*The Castle 1892*
31005

The builders of Warwick Castle recognised that a cliff overlooking a river was the ideal site for a defensive stronghold, and they took full advantage of it, as this photograph emphasises. However, the south front would not have looked like this originally: the façade is largely a Victorian creation, having been restored in 1863-66, and again in 1871 after a major fire.

**WARWICK,** *The Castle, the Courtyard 1892* 31009

The castle's fortifications are mainly the work of the Beauchamps, who acquired the earldom in 1268. Two great towers dominate; the one pictured here is Guy's Tower, while the other is Caesar's Tower, which was begun in about 1345 by Thomas Beauchamp. His son, another Thomas, built Guy's Tower around 50 years later. It is dodecagonal, with five storeys and a secret staircase.

**WARWICK,** *The Castle, the Portcullis c1900* W31301

The castle's defences were formidable. In addition to the towers and curtain walls built by the Beauchamps, it possessed a moat, drawbridge, barbican and portcullis, followed by a long passageway to the inner courtyard. Attackers trying to get from the outer to the inner gateway faced an almost suicidally hazardous task.

**WARWICK**
*The Castle, the Cedar Drawing Room c1900*
W31303

The largest of three drawing rooms, this one takes its name from the ornate cedar-wood panelling. Like all the state rooms, it was restored after the Civil War, probably around 1670. It has outstandingly rich decoration and furnishings, including three Van Dyck portraits, five Waterford chandeliers, an Aubusson carpet and a unique red-and-white marble mantelpiece by Robert Adam.

**WARWICK,** *The Old Bridge 1922* 72369

Constant repairs were needed to the medieval Great Bridge. In c1790 the Earl of Warwick offered to pay most of the cost of a new bridge, which was to be erected upstream. This was agreed, and so Castle Bridge was built, the castle grounds were extended and the old road below the castle walls was closed. Great Bridge collapsed in 1795, but its remains are still visible from Castle Bridge.

**AN ORDNANCE SURVEY MAP** *showing Warwick and surrounding areas 1886*

## WARWICK
### *High Street 1922* 72343

Visitors to Warwick sometimes wonder why it has comparatively few timber-framed buildings. The answer is that a great fire raged through the town in 1694, reducing it to 'a heap of rubbish', to quote Daniel Defoe. With most of its timber buildings destroyed, Warwick was subsequently rebuilt in brick and stone. This is most apparent along Jury Street and High Street (one continuous street), where the neo-classical Warwick Arms Hotel is just one of many fine stone buildings. It remains unchanged today from this photograph, except that the entrance canopy has been removed. However, the canopy was not original, having been erected in 1908.

▼ **WARWICK,** *Bridge End 1922* 72355

Bridge End is on the south bank of the Avon, where all the roads from the south previously met to cross into Warwick. It grew into a thriving suburb, but was isolated at the end of the 18th century when Great Bridge was superseded by Castle Bridge and the roads were realigned. This allowed Bridge End to remain mostly untouched by any future development.

► **WARWICK**
*Bridge End c1955*
W31053

Bridge End may have escaped major development, but the house on the right is a 20th-century addition, built onto the end of the terrace (compare this photograph with 72355, above). And nowhere escapes modernisation. It has been relatively minimal at Bridge End, but even so, TV aerials and burglar alarms now proliferate, along with new porches, traditionally styled but built of modern materials.

◄ **WARWICK**
*East Gate 1922* 72349

East Gate is one of three original gates into town. It was reconstructed in the early 15th century, when St Peter's Chapel was built on top, and again in 1788. The Porridge Pot, on the left of the picture, is a timber-framed building; it survived the 1694 fire, but it was re-fronted in brick in about 1700. The fake beams visible here were painted on later. It became the Porridge Pot restaurant in 1912, but now trades as Pizza Organic. It has been sensitively restored, with the fake beams painted over. The unconvincing building next door still retains its fake beams, though these are not painted on; they are non-structural timbers, added in 1856. The house behind the façade dates from c1630.

► **WARWICK**
*The Lord Leycester Hospital 1892* 31025

This delightful medieval building has been reconstructed more than once, notably in 1571 when Robert Dudley, Earl of Leicester, transformed the former guild house into a 'hospital' (almshouse) for old and disabled 'brethren' - usually ex-servicemen. It still serves this function, though it has been restored and remodelled internally.

► **WARWICK**
*The Shakespeare Restaurant 1892*
31033

Built in the 1630s, this is one of the few timber-framed buildings to have survived the 1694 fire. The travel agent Lunn Poly now occupies the greater part of it. The ground floor has been altered very slightly, but the upper floors are externally unchanged. The other buildings in this scene have undergone various degrees of modernisation, ranging from just-about-acceptable to downright disastrous.

◄ **WARWICK**
*Guy's Cliffe House from the River 1892* 31036

In the Middle Ages, the legendary Guy of Warwick retired to live as a hermit in a cave above the River Avon. A chapel was later built on the site, and a modest house was built close by. In c1750 the property was sold to Samuel Greatheed, who extended the house and gave it a neo-Palladian façade. Further alterations were carried out by his son, Bertie Greatheed, who was determined to make it worthy of its romantic setting. In 1826 the house passed to the Percy family and further alterations were made, resulting in the house we see here. Guy's Cliffe House was sold in 1946. Tragically, it has since been allowed to fall into ruin.

24

▲ **WARWICK,** *Guy's Cliffe Mill 1892* 31039

Long known as Saxon Mill, it stands upstream from Guy's Cliffe House, and was rebuilt in 1822 on a site occupied by a mill for at least 800 years. The balcony was added later to enhance the view of the mill from the mansion. Milling ceased in 1938, and in 1952 Saxon Mill was linked to an adjacent granary to form a restaurant and pub.

◄ **WARWICK**
*Guy's Cliffe Mill,
the View Upstream
1892* 31040

Once Bertie Greatheed had remodelled Guy's Cliffe House to his satisfaction, it became a favourite resort not only for his own guests but also for artists and casual visitors. There is no public access to the grounds now, but tantalising glimpses are available from a footpath which passes Saxon Mill and crosses the river on a bridge close to the point shown in the photograph.

**LEAMINGTON SPA**
*The Town Hall and
the Parade c1955*
L25047C

As Leamington grew in popularity as a spa, it became obvious that expansion was vital. A new town was laid out between 1810 and 1830, with the Parade as its main street. The town hall was added in 1882-84, but it compares unfavourably with the restrained elegance of its neighbours, such as the Regent Hotel, the white building on the left in this view.

**LEAMINGTON SPA,** *The Parade 1932* 85202

The Regent Hotel (on the left) was opened by John Williams in 1819 as Williams' Hotel. Illustrious visitors included the Prince Regent, who granted permission for its renaming, and the Duchess of Kent, with her daughter Victoria, the future queen. The Regent closed in 1999. It is been transformed into Regent Court, comprising 'retail units and luxury apartments'.

**LEAMINGTON SPA**
*The Railway Bridge 1892* 30986

Leamington acquired its first train services in 1844 when a line to Coventry was provided, with a station at Milverton. Since then, more stations and lines have been built, extended, closed and demolished, but Leamington still has good train services. This bridge takes the main line over the River Leam and the New River Walk (see 30983) on the edge of the town centre.

**LEAMINGTON SPA,** *New River Walk 1892* 30983

The picnicking children in this scene would find the site less peaceful today, blighted as it is by incessant traffic noise. Nevertheless, it is popular with dog walkers and joggers, and provides a green corridor along which people can walk to school, work or shops. It is part of a longer riverside path linking Leamington with Warwick, and part also of the 100-mile Centenary Way.

▼ **LEAMINGTON SPA,** *Spencer Street 1892* 30950

In 1836, Spencer Street was just a rough track when it was chosen as the site for a Congregationalist chapel. The chapel, second left in this picture, cost £6,000 and is an imposing neo-Classical structure. It was later used by the United Reformed Church, and then as a saleroom. It appears disused today, and Spencer Street itself is noisy and congested.

▶ **LEAMINGTON SPA**
*Jephson Gardens c1955*
L25044

The gardens were created in 1846 from the former Newbold Meadows, donated in 1836 by Edward Willes of Newbold Comyn. They were named in tribute to another Leamington benefactor, Dr Henry Jephson. A highly impressive restoration project was carried out between 2000 and 2004 by Warwick District Council, supported by the Heritage Lottery Fund.

◄ **LEAMINGTON SPA**
*The Parish Church from Victoria Bridge 1892* 30963

All Saints' Church was built in the mid-19th century, but it had already been extended before this picture was taken in 1892. Further alterations and additions followed, and in 1902 it acquired a tall bell tower which greatly enhances its appearance. The small building on the right was the cabmen's hut, where they sheltered in bad weather in the days of horse-drawn cabs.

► **WHITNASH**
*The Village 1922*
72483

Whitnash's foundation pre-dates that of Leamington, yet by 1922 it was still a peaceful village with farms, cottages, a windmill and a population probably not much in excess of 500. Since then, Whitnash has merged with Leamington, but it is also a town in its own right, designated in 1977 when its population reached 6,000.

**◄ KENILWORTH**
*The Castle 1892* 30933

One of the finest castle ruins in the UK, Kenilworth began as a timber fort. The first stone castle was built c1120 by Geoffrey de Clinton, chamberlain and treasurer to Henry I. Since then, it has been associated with some of the most famous names in British history, including Simon de Montfort, Henry V, Henry VIII and Elizabeth I.

### ◄ WHITNASH
*St Margaret's Church 1922*
72485

Except for the tower, St Margaret's was largely rebuilt 1855-80 to the design of Sir George Gilbert Scott. It contains acclaimed carvings by a local woman, Agnes Bonham, and the west window of 1876 was designed by another local woman, Ruth Young. There is a memorial brass in the chancel to Benedict Medley (died 1503) who was Clerk of the Signet to Henry VII.

▲ **KENILWORTH,** *The Castle, Leicester Buildings from the Inner Court 1922*  72412

Kenilworth began its transformation from bleak fortress to luxurious palace in the 1360s when it became the property of John of Gaunt, Duke of Lancaster. However, it was Robert Dudley, Earl of Leicester, who completed the process two centuries later after Elizabeth I gave him the castle in 1563. He remodelled the old apartments and added an extensive range of imposing new buildings.

### ◄ KENILWORTH
*The Castle c1955*
K5007

This is the keep, built in 1162. A century later, Kenilworth was involved in the Barons' War between Henry III and a rebel group of barons led by Simon de Montfort. In 1266, rebel forces were besieged in the castle for six months - the longest siege in English history. The keep survived that, but it was unable to withstand the assault of Oliver Cromwell in 1642.

## KENILWORTH
*The Old Priory,*
*the Churchyard 1892*
30947

In c1120 Geoffrey de Clinton founded a priory of Augustinian canons at Kenilworth. Over the years, gifts of land from various patrons turned St Mary's Priory into one of the wealthiest landowners in the county. In 1447 its importance was recognised by the Pope, who raised it to the status of an abbey. In the 1530s Henry VIII dissolved the monasteries and St Mary's Abbey was signed over to the king. Most of the buildings were dismantled, and their stone re-used elsewhere. However, substantial traces remain, both in the open spaces of Abbey Fields and within the churchyard around St Nicholas's Church. The photograph shows the remains of the gatehouse, formerly the main entrance to the abbey.

**KENILWORTH**
*Abbey Fields c1960*
K5053

St Mary's Abbey was surrounded by extensive grounds, most of which became sheep pasture after the Dissolution. Some of that land survives today as Abbey Fields, a valuable area of green space bounded by some of Kenilworth Old Town's finest streets and overlooked by the castle. It contains sports facilities, a children's playground and the lovely Abbey Pool.

**KENILWORTH,** *Abbey Fields, the Swimming Pool c1965* K5098

Abbey Fields is dissected by Finham Brook and Inchford Brook. The canons developed a series of pools along Finham Brook to provide water power for their mills, as well as fish and fowl for food. Today, only Abbey Pool survives, but this popular swimming pool, which opened in 1896, also perpetuates the watery theme.

**KENILWORTH**
*The Church, from the North West 1892*
30946a

The church of St Nicholas stands at the north-east corner of Abbey Fields. It was built c1190 and later remodelled in the Perpendicular style, but it suffered a typically insensitive Victorian restoration in 1864. It has one superb feature: what Pevsner describes as 'the most sumptuous Norman doorway in Warwickshire'.

**KENILWORTH,** *The Abbey Hotel 1892* 30948

This splendid pile was built in about 1885, and stands in a prominent position overlooking Abbey Fields. No longer a hotel, it is divided into flats and called simply The Abbey. In its heyday it was popular with actors appearing at the Coventry Hippodrome: Stan Laurel, Oliver Hardy and Clark Gable are just three famous names said to have been familiar with the Abbey Hotel.

▶ **KENILWORTH**
*Composite View
c1965* K5103

It is interesting to note that mostly modern scenes were chosen for this postcard issued in the 1960s. Talisman Square (top left) was still new and presumably a source of pride to some, but many did, and still do, consider it an affront. It is easy to imagine what Sir Walter Scott, the author of *The Talisman*, might think about it.

◀ **STONELEIGH**
*The Abbey 1892* 30993

Pevsner describes Stoneleigh Abbey as 'the grandest, most dramatic Georgian mansion of Warwickshire', but he also comments that it is 'mighty rather than festive', and this photograph illustrates his point admirably. It shows the west wing, designed by Francis Smith of Warwick and completed in 1726. A Cistercian abbey was founded on this site in 1154, and the present house has developed in stages from that first building. From 1561 until 1990 Stoneleigh Abbey belonged to the Leigh family, to whom the novelist Jane Austen was related. She visited the abbey in 1806 with her mother. From 1997 to 2003 Stoneleigh Abbey was the subject of a major restoration project, and it is now open to visitors.

▲ **STONELEIGH,** *The View from the Bridge 1892* 30995

It is difficult to be certain which of Stoneleigh's several bridges the caption refers to. In fact, it is difficult even to be sure which river this is, for Stoneleigh is where the Avon and the Sowe have their confluence. The most likely candidate is Stoneleigh Bridge, an elegant structure spanning the River Sowe and designed by Sir John Rennie in 1840.

◄ **STONELEIGH**
*St Mary's Church c1960*
S207002

St Mary's contains a monument to Alice Leigh, Duchess Dudley (1578-1668), who married Sir Robert Dudley, an illegitimate son of Elizabeth's I's Sir Robert Dudley, Earl of Leicester. Robert junior deserted Alice, running off to Italy with his lover, Elizabeth Southwell. But Alice had the last laugh: Charles I granted her the Dudley estates and created her a duchess in her own right.

▶ **STONELEIGH**
*Thatched Cottages*
*c1960* S207004

What an idyllic scene this is, and Stoneleigh remains a good-looking village, despite modernisation, traffic and a rather perilous proximity to Coventry. As it lies outside the ring road it may yet escape engulfment, though many residents are unhappy at the expansion of nearby Coventry Airport, from which thomsonfly.com now operates low-cost flights.

▲ **STONELEIGH**
*Birmingham Road c1960* S207007

For centuries, Stoneleigh was home to the dozens of estate workers employed by the Leighs. Today, as might be expected from somewhere which boasts both a Birmingham Road and a Coventry Road, it is largely a commuter village. The houses in this scene are typical of Stoneleigh, which retains a pleasant mixture of brick, timber and local red sandstone.

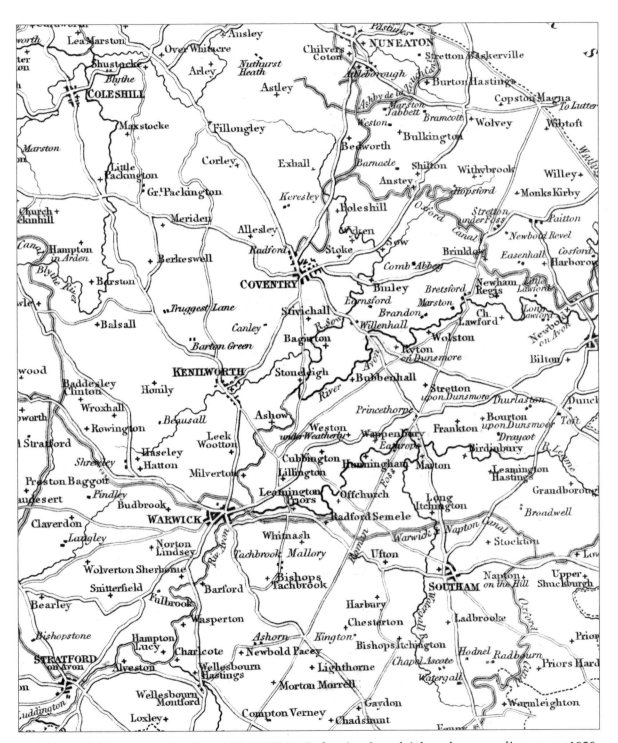

**A SECTION OF A WARWICKSHIRE COUNTY MAP** *showing Stoneleigh and surrounding areas c1850*

### ASHOW
*The Church and the Bridge 1892* 30996

The Church of the Assumption of Our Lady has a lovely riverside setting, though this appealing bridge has been somewhat modernised with new timbers. The church register begins in 1733, considerably later than most Warwickshire parishes: it is said (though it may be apocryphal) that a parish clerk called Thomas Badhams cut up the earlier volumes to make pipe spills.

# SHAKESPEARE COUNTRY AND THE LOWER AVON VALLEY

**STRATFORD UPON AVON**
*The River Avon 1892* 31041

This tranquil scene would be little changed today if only the road on the right were not now so car-choked. At least Holy Trinity Church still presides majestically over the scene. However, even there, all is not well: restoration work has long been needed, and in January 2004 the situation worsened with the discovery of death watch beetle and dry rot in the chancel. The Friends of Holy Trinity are hoping to raise £150,000 for the necessary work. Beyond the church, by the riverbank, Lucy's Mill is just visible in this photograph. This ancient mill, recorded in *Domesday Book*, was restored by Thomas Lucy in 1819. It was demolished in the 1970s and replaced by an ugly block of flats.

**STRATFORD UPON AVON,** *Holy Trinity Church and the Locks 1892* 31044

The Avon was made navigable between Stratford and Tewkesbury in 1639, but restoration was required by the 20th century. This was achieved from Tewkesbury to Evesham by 1962, and from Evesham to Stratford by 1974. Stratford New Lock was restored in 1971, and again in 1986, when it was renamed Colin P Witter Lock after a local benefactor.

**STRATFORD UPON AVON,** *The Town Centre 1892* 31074

This is just about recognisable as High Street, looking down towards its junction with Bridge Street. All of High Street's buildings were originally timber-framed, but many were re-fronted in fashionable brick or stucco in the 18th century. During the 20th century several were restored to their original appearance, while others had fake beams imposed upon them.

## STRATFORD UPON AVON
### *Shakespeare's House 1892*  31059

This is where William Shakespeare was born in 1564. Visitors to the house should not imagine they are getting an authentic experience. When the house was saved for the nation in the 19th century, its neighbours were pulled down because it was considered it should stand in isolation. Then its barns, outhouses, piggeries and brewhouse were demolished to provide space for a garden. Finally, the house itself, much altered over the centuries and seriously dilapidated, had to be restored to its original design; since nobody knew what that was, the restoration was based on romantic ideals, folk memories and a drawing made in 1769.

**STRATFORD UPON AVON,** *The Royal Shakespeare Theatre c1965*  S216164

In 1879 Stratford acquired a striped, turreted, gabled fantasy known as the Shakespeare Memorial Theatre. Mercifully, some might say, it burned down in 1926. A new Memorial Theatre opened in 1932, incorporating surviving parts of its predecessor. It was renamed the Royal Shakespeare Theatre in 1961. In 1986, a second theatre, the Swan, was created in the remains of the 1879 building, as seen in this picture.

**STRATFORD UPON AVON,** *Tudor House 1892* 31060A

This fine timber-framed building stands on the corner of Ely Street and High Street and remains virtually unchanged, although it is now occupied by Pizza Hut and Supa Snaps. It displays the use of close studding, a construction method which uses more timber than is actually required, either for decorative effect or simply to demonstrate the owner's wealth.

**STRATFORD UPON AVON,** *The River Avon 1922* 72395

Boating has long been a popular pursuit for visitors to Stratford, and for many residents too. Colourful boats throng the river and canal daily, but none is as glamorous as the Venetian gondola (complete with gondolier) imported by the novelist Marie Corelli, who lived in Stratford from 1899 until her death in 1924.

**STRATFORD UPON AVON,** *Harvard House 1922* 72384

This house was built in 1595-96 by Thomas Rogers, whose grandson, John Harvard, settled in America, and died there in 1638, bequeathing money towards the establishment of Harvard College. Compare this picture to 31074 (on page 43), in which Harvard House is on the left. The ground floor was rebuilt c1900, as part of a restoration project in which the novelist Marie Corelli was instrumental.

### SHOTTERY
*The Village 1922*
72399

This is Tavern Lane, from which two footpaths lead across playing fields to Stratford. Shakespeare must have used these paths in the days when he was courting Anne Hathaway. This is still the best way to travel between Shottery and Stratford, especially as the traffic which blights other Shottery streets is denied access to Tavern Lane.

**SHOTTERY,** *Anne Hathaway's Cottage 1922*  72403

The 'cottage' is actually a substantial farmhouse, known as Hewlands Farm in Anne Hathaway's time. The earliest part of the building is supported by cruck beams dating from the 1460s. It belonged to Anne's family from 1543 until 1838, when it was sold by William Taylor, a descendant of Anne's brother Bartholomew. However, the family continued in residence because William's daughter, Mary Baker, was engaged as the resident custodian (the cottage had already been open to visitors before the sale). In 1893 the Shakespeare Birthplace Trust acquired the cottage and Mary continued to act as custodian until her death in 1899. Her son, William Hathaway Baker, succeeded her in the post.

**SHOTTERY**
*Anne Hathaway's
Cottage,
the Parlour 1912*
65144

When the Birthplace
Trust acquired the
cottage it removed
any of the Hathaways'
possessions and
furnishings it considered
inappropriate, including
a Victorian grate which
had been inserted into
this open fireplace. The
wooden settle is believed
to have been there since
Anne's day, and was
once popularly known as
the 'courting settle'.

**SHOTTERY,** *Anne Hathaway's Cottage, an Old Bedstead 1912* 65147

This is the grandest of the four beds in the cottage, but it does not look very comfortable. The mattress is short and rather narrow for a double bed (though it is obviously intended as a double), and is supported by a sagging framework of rope. A painting of this same scene, almost identical to the photograph, hangs in the cottage. Dated 1890, it is signed by Fred Roe.

**SHOTTERY,** *Anne Hathaway's Cottage, the Buttery 1913* 65149

The sparsely furnished buttery remains unchanged. The main purpose of a buttery was generally the storage of food and drink, making it similar to what later became known as a larder. However, it is possible that this was also where the Hathaways (or their servants) churned milk from their own cattle into creamy butter.

**SHOTTERY,** *At Shottery Brook c1890* S297546

The footbridge has been replaced by a more substantial structure, and there are formal paths beside the brook, but little else has changed in this scene - except, of course, that women no longer have to collect water from the brook, though Shottery residents did rely on it for their supply long after Stratfordians had acquired piped water. Anne Hathaway's Cottage can be seen in the background, and a beautifully printed copy of this superb photograph hangs in the cottage. There is also a painting in the cottage showing a similar scene, made by Ebenezer Wake Cook in 1893.

### SHOTTERY
*Washing Day c1890*
S297548

In these days of labour-saving machines, it is easy to forget how very tedious domestic chores must once have been. Ironically, items similar to the stool, tub and basket in this picture can now be found, well buffed with wax polish, in local antique shops, where they are bought by people who may never have hand-washed an item of clothing in their entire lives.

**WILMCOTE,** *Mary Arden's House c1955*  W216004

This 16th-century farmhouse belongs to the Shakespeare Birthplace Trust. It was previously believed to have been the home of William Shakespeare's mother, Mary Arden, before her marriage to John Shakespeare. In 2000 it was discovered that Mary had actually lived next door, at Glebe Farm. Fortunately, the Trust already owned that one too, so it was renamed Mary Arden's House and this one became Palmer's Farm.

► **CHARLECOTE**
*Charlecote Park,
from the Upper
Gardens c1884*
17112

The Lucy family
owned Charlecote
from c1200 until
1945 when they gave
it to the National
Trust, though the
family still lives
there. The present
house was begun in
1558, but has been
much altered since.
It has had its share
of illustrious visitors,
including Elizabeth I
in 1572, and Charles I
in 1642, shortly before
the Battle of Edgehill.

◄ **MORETON PADDOX**
*The Fountain c1955* M138001

The neo-Jacobean house Moreton
Paddox was built in the village of
Moreton Morrell between 1909 and
1915 for Major and Mrs Robert Emmett
by the architect W H Romaine-Walker,
who specialised in substantial country
houses of this type. No expense was
spared, and the gardens were as
magnificent as the house, with a formal
'canal' flanked by gravelled paths and
tightly trimmed hedges. But steadily
increasing maintenance costs meant that
in 1944 the house had to be put on the
market. It subsequently belonged to the
Birmingham Co-operative Society and
then the Workers' Travel Association. In
1959 it was demolished, though some
ancillary buildings survive as a stud farm.

▲ **MORETON PADDOX,** *The Staircase c1955* M138006

Moreton Paddox featured profuse neo-Jacobean decoration in wood and plaster in most areas, including the main staircase, as we see here. But other periods featured too: the stone-vaulted chapel was Gothic, and the bedrooms were decorated in an assortment of 17th- and 18th-century styles.

◄ **MORETON PADDOX**
*The Ballroom c1955*
M138005

The creators of the impressive neo-Jacobean panelling probably never expected that it would one day be partnered with a set of utilitarian chairs that would look more at home in a village hall.

◀ **WESTON-ON-AVON**
*The Village c1955*
W498051

Weston is a tiny village, little more than a cluster of cottages leading to a 15th-century church at the end of a no through road. This lovely cottage has been unusually fortunate in its owners: fifty years after the photograph was taken, the cottage remains virtually unaltered. It has been re-thatched, but care has been taken to replicate the design seen here.

◄ **MORETON PADDOX**
*The Lounge*
*c1955* M138008

The large windows were essential in a room which contained so much dark panelling. Even so, it must have felt gloomy at times, and the functional mid-20th-century furniture does nothing to improve matters, looking ugly and incongruous in such a setting.

▲ **WELFORD-ON-AVON,** *Tenpenny Cottage and the Church c1960* W213087

There can be few people in Britain who have not seen a photograph of this scene at some time or other, consciously or not. Scarcely a year goes by that it does not feature on at least one calendar, biscuit tin or jigsaw. The cottage has acquired new windows and a coat of paint on the chimney stack since this photograph was taken, but remains otherwise unchanged.

◄ **WELFORD-ON-AVON**
*The Church c1960*
W213081

St Peter's is built of blue lias, the distinctive local stone. It has several interesting features, including splendid stained glass, some of it modern, and a font which is said to be Saxon. The lychgate shown in this picture was said to be the oldest in Warwickshire, but it was replaced in c1970.

**WELFORD-ON-AVON,** *The Maypole c1960* W213054

Welford has had a maypole since the 14th century; the present glossy red, white and blue pole
was installed in 1967 and refurbished in 2003. The pole is topped by a weathervane featuring a
running fox on a golden ball.

### WELFORD-ON-AVON
*Boat Lane c1960*
W213043

Boat Lane leads to a former ferry crossing. There used to be many ferries on the Avon, but the modern habit of driving everywhere has ensured that none now survives in Warwickshire, other than a seasonal one at Stratford, which is essentially for the enjoyment and convenience of tourists, serving no significant practical purpose.

**WELFORD-ON-AVON,** *Ancient Lights c1960* W213041

A 'light' in this context is a window, and upstairs is an unmistakably genuine ancient light, an iron casement set in a wooden frame, with an iron stay dangling below. This was characteristic of the Midlands vernacular, but most have been replaced with ugly modern windows. It is still possible to have casements made by a blacksmith, but few householders choose that option.

▼ **WELFORD-ON-AVON,** *Chapel Street, Old Cottages c1955* W213019

Welford has spread enormously since 1955. A fair number of old cottages still line the earliest village streets around the church, but elsewhere any surviving cottage tends to be islanded in a sea of modernity. But several still survive on Chapel Street, including this thatched row of four.

► **WELFORD-ON-AVON**
*The Bridge and the River Avon c1960*
W213050

This is part of Binton Bridges, linked bridges which span the Avon between Welford and Binton by way of mid-stream islands. The parish boundary runs along the river, and was formerly the county boundary too, for Welford was in Gloucestershire until 1931.

◄ **WELFORD-ON-AVON**
*The River and the Church c1960*
W213053

This viewpoint must be just outside Welford on the Bidford road, where the land rises slightly. The exact viewpoint is inaccessible now, but looking towards Welford from a nearby site reveals a less pleasing view, with a factory-like farm building looming large.

▶ **BIDFORD-ON-AVON**
*The Bridge 1899*
44127

In Saxon times this was Byda's Ford, where the Roman Ryknild Street forded the Avon. It is not known exactly when the bridge was built, but it was probably some time in the 15th century. It can take only a single flow of vehicles, so a clutter of traffic lights and signs spoils its appearance today.

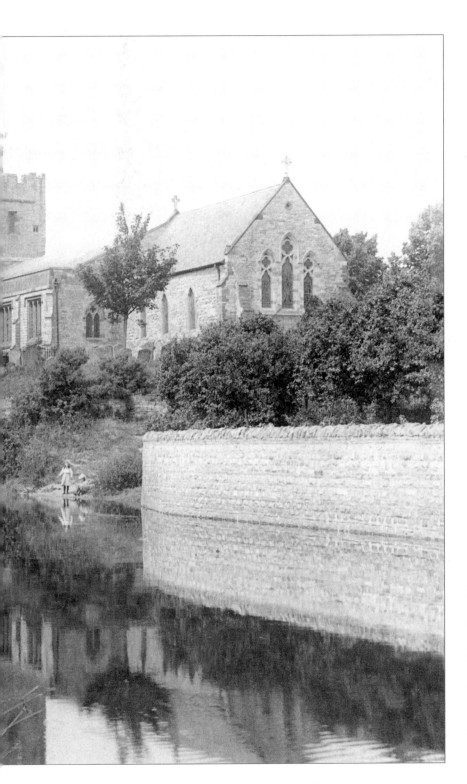

**BIDFORD-ON-AVON**
*The Church 1899*  44131

This 1899 view conveys a feeling of tranquillity which has been lost from Bidford today, but at least St Laurence's Church still benefits from an attractive setting, its 13th-century tower dominating the village when one views it from the bridge or the riverbank.

**BIDFORD-ON-AVON**
*High Street 1910* 62641

Second from left in this view
is the Mason's Arms Inn,
which is now the Dilshad,
an Indian restaurant. The
owners have carefully
preserved its fine façade
and lovely windows, but the
buildings further along the
street have fared less well,
while the attractive shop to
the Dilshad's left has been
demolished to make way for
a new road.

▶ **BIDFORD-ON-AVON**
*The Village 1901*
47340

Shakespeare knew this 16th-century stone building as the Falcon Inn, and is reputed to have drunk there. Presumably, it was still in business in 1901, because the men sitting in the road outside all have tankards in front of them. The inn has since been converted into private homes, and anybody hanging around in the road these days would soon be squashed by traffic.

◀ **BIDFORD-ON-AVON**
*The River and Bell Court Cottage c1955*
B91021

Though by no means unchanged, this riverside house is still recognisable and has an enviable situation. Bell Court was originally the name of one of the six manors which made up medieval Bidford. The others were Bidford itself, Bidford Grange, and the outlying hamlets of Broom, Barton and Marlcliff.

▲ **BIDFORD-ON-AVON,** *Marlcliff 1901*  47337

About a mile from Bidford, the hamlet of Marlcliff sits snugly below the eponymous marl cliff beside the River Avon. There are a few 17th-century cottages here, whose residents are usually outnumbered by the anglers who throng the riverbank.

◄ **MARSTON**
*The Inn 1901*  47347

There are several Marstons in Warwickshire, but the date and reference number of this print suggest Long Marston, a commuter village which has expanded enormously since 1901. It is just about feasible that this charming little pub could be concealed within the fabric of the present-day Mason's Arms, but it is just as likely that it has been demolished.

**SALFORD PRIORS,** *The Church 1901* 47330

Place names are sometimes misleading, but Salford Priors is exactly what it sounds like: a village which developed by a ford on a salt way and belonged to a priory - in this case, St Mary's Priory (later St Mary's Abbey) at Kenilworth. Salford was given to St Mary's in 1122; before that it belonged to the monastery at Evesham, and was known as Salteford Major.

### ABBOT'S SALFORD
*The Nunnery 1901*
47331

Originally Salteford Minor, Abbot's Salford was re-named after a 15th-century Abbot of Evesham built a timber-framed country house there, part of which survives as the west wing of this building, which dates mostly from c1600. It served as a nunnery between 1807 and 1838, but is now the Salford Hall Hotel.

**ABBOT'S SALFORD,** *The Nunnery 1901* 47332

The dome-shaped baskets in the recess are bee skeps, in which honeybees were housed before the invention of wooden hives. Skeps were usually woven from straw, but grass, reed or sedge might be used, depending on local availability. The ancient Egyptians used similar skeps, but the oldest surviving evidence of British use is a 12th-century skep found in York.

# ALCESTER, HENLEY AND THE FORMER FOREST OF ARDEN

**ALCESTER,** *The Town Hall c1965* A113043

Officially known as Alcester War Memorial Town Hall, this building actually has no municipal function, having been designated a 'village hall' in 1978. It was built as a market hall in 1618, with funds provided by the lord of the manor, Sir Fulke Greville. It was purchased by public subscription in 1919 and dedicated to the memory of those who died in the First World War.

**ALCESTER**
*Butter Street c1965*
A113044

In the 16th century, the area round the churchyard was the commercial centre of Alcester; it included Butter Street, which borders two sides of the churchyard. It is a narrow street which receives very little direct sunshine, making it the ideal site for the sale of butter and other perishables.

**ALCESTER,** *Oversley Green c1965* A113051

Oversley Green is just a short walk from Alcester, beside the River Arrow, near its confluence with the River Alne. This is the Arrow, and the old stone bridge over the river is just visible. When the Alcester-Stratford road was turnpiked in 1753 a toll house was built on the Oversley side of the bridge, but it was later transferred to Hoo Mill Corner.

**WIXFORD**
*The Village 1901* 47341

How sad that these cottages
have been demolished and
a new house built. Though
traditionally styled, it will
take decades to mellow.
St Milburga's Church is still
there, and the churchyard
contains a rare Grade II
listed building, an 18th-
century horse-house made
of gorse and thatch, which
was built to provide shelter
for the mounts of visiting
clergymen. It was renovated
in 1997.

▼ **WIXFORD,** *The Village 1901*  47342

The cottage on the left retains its thatch and is still recognisable, despite having acquired some modern window-frames. Its neighbours have fared less well. Across the road from these cottages is another of Wixford's listed buildings (see 47341): a red telephone box. It must be well loved, for somebody has provided it with a carpet, and made a miniature garden outside the door.

► **HENLEY-IN-ARDEN**
*High Street 1949*
H414019

Henley is a fine example of a medieval settlement developing in linear fashion along a highway, as this photograph demonstrates - though it tells only part of the story, for the High Street is a mile long. The beautiful buildings which line the street span some seven or eight centuries, and display a glorious variety of domestic architectural styles.

◄ **HENLEY-IN-ARDEN**
*High Street c1960*
H414031

The sign for Tudor Dairy Ices (on the building second from the left) takes us back to 1893, when a Mrs Howins, who owned a grocer's shop and a milk round, started trading under that name. She eventually sold the business to Harry and Arthur Fathers, who in 1934 started to produce hand-made ice cream which became enormously popular. But in 1959 the brothers sold their award-winning business to Ross Foods, and Henley ice cream ceased to be made by hand. In 1991 Ross sold Tudor Dairies to another company, which went into receivership in 1997. But in a way, Henley ice cream lives on through Steve and Cindy Brittan's ice cream parlour on the High Street, which serves ice cream made on Midlands farms to a traditional recipe.

► **HENLEY-IN-ARDEN**
*High Street c1960*
H414030

The church of St John the Baptist was built c1450, and so was the timber-framed Guild House just visible beyond the church in this view. The Guild of Holy Trinity, St John the Evangelist and St John the Baptist engaged in works of charity, but it was dissolved in 1547. The building has served many functions since, with the lower floor now in use as a public library.

## HENLEY-IN-ARDEN
*The White Swan Hotel*
*c1960*  H414034

The White Swan dates from c1600, but there is believed to have been an inn on this site since c1350. It is said to be haunted by the ghost of a housemaid who was hanged for murder in the square outside.

**HENLEY-IN-ARDEN,** *The View from the Mount c1950*  H414011

Despite its obvious antiquity, Henley is a bit of an upstart. It was preceded by Beaudesert, founded in the 11th century when Thurstan de Montfort built a motte and bailey castle on the knoll called the Mount. His descendant Peter de Montfort was involved in the opposition of the barons to Henry III led by Simon de Montfort (no relation, apparently). After the king's triumph at the Battle of Evesham in 1265, where both de Montforts died, the town of Beaudesert which had grown up around the castle was destroyed, and subsequent development took place along what is now the High Street. A close look at this scene reveals the rooftops of the High Street running southwards from St John's Church (right).

**HENLEY-IN-ARDEN**
*The View from the Mount c1955* H414010

Like H414011 (page 74), this view reveals St John's Church and Henley High Street, but it also includes St Nicholas's Church at Beaudesert, though only the top of its tower is visible above the trees (centre). The church was built c1070 by Thurstan de Montfort. The little town of Beaudesert gained its market charter in 1140, while Henley had to wait until 1449.

**HENLEY-IN-ARDEN,** *St Nicholas's Church, the Interior c1960* H414043

This superb Norman chancel arch, with its elaborate carvings, is considered the finest feature of St Nicholas's Church. The Norman south doorway also survives, with a zigzag-patterned arch. The church tower was added in the 15th century. Beaudesert is still a separate parish, distinct from Henley.

◀ **CLAVERDON**
*Country Stores and
the Post Office c1960*
C253001

One would think a village
the size of Claverdon
could support two general
stores, but modern
villagers prefer to drive
to a superstore rather
than walk to the corner
shop. This shop is no
longer trading, though
another general stores
further along the road is
still clinging on. The post
office is now located in a
butcher's shop.

◄ **CLAVERDON**
*The Green*
*c1960* C253012

Claverdon is a large village which saw considerable expansion in the 1970s and is mostly inhabited by commuters. It is believed that the medieval village was enclosed within a deer park in 1300, but the only clue to that nowadays is the name of Park Farm, near the church.

▲ **CLAVERDON,** *The Church c1960* C253014

Dedicated to St Michael and All Angels, the church contains monuments to the Galton family of Edstone Hall. Sir Francis Galton FRS (1822-1911) was the man who discovered that each individual has unique fingerprints. There are also some early monuments to the Spencer family, ancestors of the late Diana, Princess of Wales.

◄ **CLAVERDON**
*The Forge c1960*
C253007

In 1960 the forge was owned by Robin Lomas, who had stopped shoeing horses in 1954 to specialise in wrought iron tools and implements. He then began a taxi service and sold petrol supplied by Esso. In 1981 a farrier bought the forge and resumed the shoeing of horses. Today, the forge is owned by K and L Sparkes, aptly named 'purveyors of stoves and chimneys'.

THE VILLAGE

INTERIOR OF CHUR

THE BELL AND MEMORIAL

TANWORTH I

THE CHURCH

RDEN

THE VILLAGE

TIA.16.

## TANWORTH-IN-ARDEN
### *Composite View c1965*
T124016

It was originally just Tanworth, but the suffix was added in the 19th century to avoid confusion with Tamworth, which is now in Staffordshire but was then in Warwickshire. Modern houses proliferate in Tanworth now, but the old chestnut tree (glimpsed top left) still casts a shade over the green, and the Bell Inn (top and bottom left), across the road from the green, is still in business.

► **ULLENHALL**
*Composite View*
*c1965* U19011

The most striking thing about present-day Ullenhall is the number of houses with names such as The Old Central Stores, The Old Bakery, The Old Post Office and The Old Forge, to name but a few. The former Perry Mill is now dwarfed by a modern extension, but Perry Mill Lane (bottom right) remains pleasantly rural, in contrast to the ugly, traffic-calmed lane from Henley.

ST. MARY THE VIRGIN CHURCH

GREETINGS FROM

THE VILLAGE

ULLENHALL

WHITE COTTAGE AND WAR MEMORIAL

THE PERRY MILL

◄ **STUDLEY**
*The Manor House*
*c1960* S299017a

This beautiful 17th-century building appears to have been called New Hall in 1725, when it belonged to Thomas Chambers of Gorcott Hall (three miles north of Studley). It is now called Mountbatten House after Lord Louis Mountbatten, who was president of the Royal Life Saving Society, which moved its headquarters here in 1980.

▲ **STUDLEY,** *Studley College c1960* S299017d

Studley Castle was designed by Samuel Beazley and built between 1834 and 1837 for Francis Lyttleton Holyoake Goodricke. In 1903 it was sold to Frances Evelyn, Countess of Warwick, who turned it into a horticultural college for women. It continued in this capacity until 1969, when it became a training centre for British Leyland, and it was later used as a marketing institute and conference centre by the Rover Group.

◀ **STUDLEY**
*The Barley Mow c1960*
S299017c

Samuel Lewis, compiling *A Topographical Dictionary of England* in 1831, described the Barley Mow as 400 years old even then. It seems to have originally been a granary used by the monks of Studley Priory, but in 1534 they converted it to an inn to cater for travellers. It has been much altered and extended since.

# EASTERN WARWICKSHIRE
# AND THE COTSWOLD FRINGE

**BRINKLOW,** *Broad Street c1955* B689005

Brinklow was one of 400 new towns deliberately created between 1066 and 1349, when the Black Death brought an end to the practice. Like many of them, Brinklow never really took off. It was 1790 before the construction of the Oxford Canal, with a wharf at Brinklow, brought real prosperity. Brinklow is town-sized today, but it is basically a commuter village.

### RUGBY
*The Market Place, High Street and Sheep Street 1932*
85179

Rugby gained its market charter in 1255; the market took place in both the Market Place and neighbouring Sheep Street until 1953, when it was transferred initially to Church Street, then to Gas Street. It is back in the Market Place now, on Mondays, Fridays and Saturdays. In addition, a farmers' market is held on the last Thursday of each month.

**RUGBY,** *Junction of High Street and Sheep Street 1922* 72119

Nowadays, new estates or developments have streets named according to some irrelevant theme - anything from Cumbrian lakes to South American countries. But ancient names such as High Street, Sheep Street and Market Place tell us what these streets were for, or what happened there; in other words, they tell us something about the history of Rugby, which also has a Wooll Street (off Sheep Street).

**RUGBY**
*North Street 1922*  72127

North Street was mainly residential in the early 20th century, with some splendid houses, including thatched cottages. They became derelict in the 1920s and were demolished in 1933. Similarly, a bow-fronted Regency house was demolished in 1930 and a six-bay Georgian house went in 1953. This mock-Tudor pub survives. It was the Old Inn in 1922, but is now the Crown.

**RUGBY**
*St Andrew's Parish Church 1922* 72131

St Andrew's Church was rebuilt between 1877 and 1885, and the east tower was added in 1895. However, the 14th-century west tower shown in this photograph is the oldest structure in Rugby. It is intriguing that St Andrew's is claimed to be the only church in the world to have two towers with ringing bells.

**RUGBY,** *Caldecott Park 1922* 72138

Just a short walk from the shopping streets, Caldecott Park is a welcome refuge from urban Rugby. It contains extensive grassed areas, some mature trees, sports facilities, a children's play area and formal planting. A range of events is held in the park on weekends throughout the summer.

### RUGBY
*The School and the Close c1965* R69079

It was during a game of football in the Close in 1823 that William Webb Ellis first picked up the ball and ran with it. The sport that was born in that impulsive moment is now enjoyed worldwide, and the Close draws many visitors who simply want to stand in that historic spot where it all began.

**RUGBY,** *The School Memorial Cross 1922* 72162

The memorial cross stands on Lawrence Sheriff Street, and was erected to the memory of those who died in the First World War. No names are inscribed on it, but there is also a war memorial chapel built in 1922 (as an adjunct to the main chapel), in which the names of hundreds of Old Rugbeians are inscribed.

## SOUTHAM
*Market Hill c1960* S298048

Southam is predominantly a dormitory town now, but it is a historic place. Roman coins have been found in the churchyard, and a market charter was granted by Henry III in 1227. It stands astride the Welsh Road used by cattle drovers, and in the early 19th century it was a stop for coaches such as the London-Warwick-Birmingham Mail, the Express and the Sovereign.

## SOUTHAM, *The Church c1965* S298063

A landmark for miles around, thanks to its tall broach spire and its commanding position on a slight hill above the River Stowe, St James's Church was almost entirely rebuilt in 1853-54. Externally, it has yet to mellow, but the interior is known for its fine clerestory.

**SOUTHAM,** *The Old Mint c1965* S298065

How sad that someone has been unable to resist renaming this 14th-century building the Olde Mint. Local tradition insists that it owes its name to an unlikely incident after the Battle of Edgehill in 1642, when Charles I is said to have come here and demanded that the local gentry donate silverware to be melted down and minted into coins so he could pay his army.

**NAPTON-ON-THE-HILL**
*On the Canal c1965* N71026b

Napton means 'settlement on the hill', so the suffix is superfluous. However, it does emphasise Napton's uniqueness as Warwickshire's only true hilltop village. Napton Hill is half-encircled by the Oxford Canal, which meets the Grand Union Canal (this stretch of which was formerly the Warwick and Napton Canal) at nearby Napton Junction.

### ▶ KINETON
### *The Memorial*
### *c1965*  K65017

For centuries Kineton was a market town, but the market ceased in 1890 and now it is just a large village. The war memorial stands on a tiny green close to the Swan Hotel (the white-painted building, centre) which dates from 1668. Kineton has several attractive cottages, some of them with the distinctive chequered brickwork seen in those on the right of this photograph.

### ◀ KINETON
### *St Peter's Church*
### *c1960*  K65013

St Peter's is one of Kineton's best features, thanks in part to the striking russet colour of the ironstone, which looks wonderful in early morning or late afternoon sunlight. The abundant Gothic pinnacles and battlements are attractive too. The nave and chancel were rebuilt in 1755 by the architect Sanderson Miller, who lived at nearby Radway Grange.

▲ **EDGE HILL,** *Edgehill Battleground 1922* 72078

It was on the escarpment of Edge Hill (in the background of this photograph) that Charles I unfurled his standard in 1642 before the first major battle of the Civil War. The actual battle took place below the escarpment in the much flatter area between Radway and Kineton. It is forbidden to visit the battlefield today because it is occupied by a Ministry of Defence depot.

◄ **EDGE HILL**
*The Walk through the Beech Woods 1922* 72075

It is believed that in 1642 there were few trees and no woods on Edge Hill. Today, Knowle End Wood, Edge Hill Wood, Castle Wood and Edgehill Covert grace the top of the escarpment, forming a continuous band of woodland nearly two miles long. These lovely beeches were planted in the 18th century, possibly by the architect Sanderson Miller.

**EDGE HILL,** *The Obelisk 1922* 72076

Two memorials to the Battle of Edgehill have been erected locally, but this is not one of them. This obelisk was raised in 1854 on the edge of Castle Wood to commemorate the Battle of Waterloo (1815). Incidentally, it is worth noting that while the escarpment is usually written as Edge Hill, the village and the battle are always written as Edgehill.

93

**EDGE HILL,** *Jacob's Ladder 1922* 72074

Jacob's Ladder is the name given to a path which climbs steeply up the escarpment between Radway and Ratley, through Castle Wood. There are several other steep paths in the UK with this name. It probably derives from the Old Testament story of Jacob's vision of a ladder linking earth to heaven.

▼ **EDGE HILL,** *The Castle Inn c1960* E102013

This building was designed in 1749 by the architect Sanderson Miller to mark the spot where the Royal standard was raised in 1642. The main tower was loosely modelled on Guy's Tower at Warwick Castle. The building was originally known as Radway Castle or Radway Tower, but it became the Castle Inn during Queen Victoria's reign.

▶ **COMPTON WYNYATES**
*The House and the Garden 1922* 72100

Compton Wynyates often used to be called Compton-in-the-Hole, which sounds unappealing but refers to the house's idyllic setting in a hollow beneath Edge Hill. The Comptons owned the manor from c1200, but the present house was built c1480-1520. It is one of the most beautiful houses in England.

◄ **COMPTON WYNYATES**
*The Garden 1922*
72098

In the late 18th century, Compton Wynyates was abandoned by its cash-strapped owner, the 8th Earl of Northampton, and narrowly avoided being pulled down. In 1851 the 3rd Marquess of Northampton inherited the property and set about restoring it and remodelling the garden. In 1895 the 5th Marquess laid out the topiary garden we see here.

► **COMPTON WYNYATES**
*The Courtyard 1922* 72104

The house consists of four ranges built round a courtyard. On the right here is the south range, which includes the parlour and great chamber. On the left is the east range, which contains the hall, marked by the splendid bay window.

**COMPTON WYNYATES,** *The Minstrels' Gallery 1922*  72106

The gallery was probably installed by William Compton, who built the present house. He served as esquire to Henry VIII, and in 1512 he was knighted after distinguishing himself at the Battle of Tournai. He was further rewarded with the ruined Fulbrook Castle near Warwick, and plundered it for materials and furnishings to use at Compton Wynyates.

**SHIPSTON-ON-STOUR,** *High Street c1960* S296016a

For centuries this 'sheep town on the Stour' was a major sheep and wool market. The trade declined in the 19th century, but Shipston continued to prosper because it was also a commercial centre for the Feldon and it lay on a busy coaching route. A couple of former coaching inns still grace its streets today, including the George Hotel, seen here on the right.

# THE COALFIELD TOWNS OF THE NORTH

**NUNEATON,** *Market Place c1945* N89010

There has been a market here for over 700 years; it still happens twice-weekly even now, with up to 115 stalls on a Wednesday, and, so it is said, a staggering 225 on a Saturday, when they spread along Bridge Street, Abbey Street and Queen's Road. There is also a farmers' market on the first Wednesday of the month.

▼ **NUNEATON,** *Church Street c1945*  N89020

Part of Church Street was destroyed in an air raid in 1941, but misguided development and unrestricted traffic growth have since done far more damage to the townscape than German bombs. The buildings in this photograph have been replaced with grotesque monstrosities, and the road seems to be permanently congested.

► **NUNEATON**
*Church Street c1945*
N89019

The building of a ring road in the 1970s led to the mass demolition of homes and shops, and this scene is unrecognisable now. Only one of these buildings remains: the one with two gable ends, just beyond the car. It was originally the Queen's Head, but is now called the Pen and Wig.

**NUNEATON**
*Bond Gate c1945*
N89022

People lived and traded on Bond Gate until 1969. Now, together with Bond Street, it is a dispiriting introduction to Nuneaton for those of us who arrive by train. All these buildings have been swept away, and replaced by a dire hotchpotch of modern horrors overlooking endless traffic. The buses now leave from an ugly new station round the corner, with a footbridge providing pedestrian access from Bond Gate.

**NUNEATON**
*Queen's Road c1945*
N89017

When Nuneaton expanded rapidly in the 1890s, Queen's Road became the principal street. The building on the right of this picture was erected in 1893, with council offices upstairs and a fire station below. The council offices became a library in 1934, but the building was demolished in 1962. Many of its neighbours were also destroyed around the same time.

◄ **NUNEATON**
*Abbey Street c1945*
N89007

The construction of the ring road cut Abbey Street in half and was accompanied by wholesale demolition. Fortunately, the distinctive range of buildings on the left has survived relatively unscathed. Completed in 1928 for Nuneaton Co-operative Society, it was refurbished in 2000 and still houses the Co-op. The Scala Theatre, on the right, has also survived. Built in 1914 as a cinema, it now houses Shipley's Amusements.

**▲ NUNEATON**
*Riversley Park c1955* N89048

Edward Melly was born in Liverpool in 1857, but came to Nuneaton after being educated at Rugby School. A mine owner, he was prominent in public life, and gave Riversley Park to the people in 1907. It took its name from the Melly family home, which overlooked the River Mersey in Liverpool.

**◄ NUNEATON**
*The Council House c1945* N89023

The Council Offices built on Queen's Road in 1893, see N89017, (page 101) replaced a Town Hall of 1818, but were themselves replaced in 1934 by this neo-Georgian pile on Coton Road. Formerly known as the Council House, it has recently been renamed the Town Hall, following the construction of a new red-brick Council House next to it.

**NUNEATON** *from the air 1961* AFA92056

**MEREVALE**
*The Church from the South 1924*  76116

The Church of Our Lady was formerly the gatehouse chapel to the Cistercian Merevale Abbey. Such chapels were provided by the Cistercians for visitors and servants. The church is noted for its glass, including some probably paid for by Henry VII in around 1500 in grateful thanks for victory at the Battle of Bosworth (1485), which was fought nearby (Bosworth is about eight miles from Merevale).

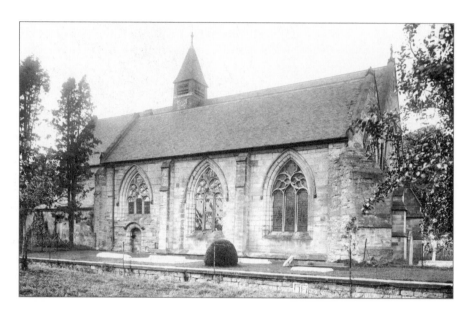

**MEREVALE,** *The Ruins 1924*  76119

Merevale Abbey was founded in 1148 by Robert, Earl Ferrers. Only fragments of the abbey survive, mostly in the grounds of Abbey Farm, next to the church. The farmhouse is itself constructed from stone reclaimed from the abbey.

**MEREVALE**
*The Ruins 1924*
76118

The historian Michael K Jones believes that the Battle of Bosworth was actually fought between Merevale and Atherstone. A contemporary source, the Croyland Chronicle, called it the Battle of Merevale. Henry VII is believed to have stayed at Merevale Abbey the night before the battle, and he later paid compensation for battle damage to the abbey and nearby villages.

**HURLEY,** *The Village c1965* H189002

Hurley began life as a small settlement in a clearing in the Forest of Arden, and it probably did not grow substantially until Dexter Colliery opened in 1927. By the time the colliery closed in 1968, there were already large council estates here; many more houses have been built since, though only a minimum of services appears to have been provided.

**KINGSBURY,** *The Church c1955* K167001

The Church of St Peter and St Paul overlooks the River Tame and was founded c1150 by Osbert de Arden. The Norman nave survives, but the chancel and tower were added in the 13th century. Some historians believe that the Saxon kings of Mercia, who had a palace at nearby Tamworth, were buried at Kingsbury Church.

108

**KINGSBURY,** *The River c1955*  K167008

Hemlingford Bridge, built in 1783, spans the River Tame a little way to the south of the church. On one side of the river is Kingsbury Water Park; on the other side are the traffic, industrial estates, oil storage depots and fridge mountain of so-called 'Kingsbury village'. The busy A4097 spans the river to the south of Hemlingford Bridge, the M42 a mile to the north.

▶ **KINGSBURY**
*The Boating Pool c1955*
K167009

What is now called Kingsbury Water Park contains 30 pools like this, set in 600 acres of the Tame Valley. The legacy of five decades of sand and gravel extraction, the water park has been open to the public since 1975. It receives over 300,000 visitors a year, mainly for bird watching, angling, walking, horse riding and water sports.

### ◄ POLESWORTH
*The River 1958* P64013

Polesworth has developed on both sides of the River Anker, with the original Saxon settlement on the north bank. The photographer in this instance was looking across to the south bank, recording for posterity a scene which no longer exists: only the bridge survives. It was built in 1776 and widened in 1924.

**POLESWORTH**
*A Thatched Cottage
c1955* P64005

This cottage (see also P64013, page 110) stood in the Square, which is just a crossroads now, but was once a focal point and meeting place, with a pub, the Chetwynd Arms. The Square now offers widened roads full of traffic, a plethora of ugly signage and street furniture, a car park, a car showroom, a fire station and some rather bleak-looking riverside green space.

**POLESWORTH,** *The Church 1924* 76123

The Abbey Church of St Editha dates from Norman times, but Polesworth Abbey is said to have been founded by King Egbert in 827. He installed his daughter (some say his sister) Editha as its first abbess. The church contains an effigy of an abbess dating from c1200. While too late to represent Editha, it is said to be the earliest effigy of an abbess in England.

## POLESWORTH
### *The Gatehouse 1924*
76124

This 14th-century gatehouse is also known as Nunnery Gate. Together with the older parts of the church, it is all that remains of the abbey. The other buildings were dismantled after the Dissolution, and the stone was used to build Polesworth Hall, which was itself demolished in the 19th century. Some of the stone was again re-used in building the present vicarage in 1868.

**POLESWORTH,** *Pooley Hall c1955*  P64007

Pooley Hall was built by Thomas Cockayne between 1506 and 1509 on the site of a much older house. It has an embattled tower with a stair turret, and is built of red brick with stone mullions and quoins. Though it is a highly unlikely story, there are said to be secret passages connecting Pooley Hall to Polesworth Abbey.

**WATER ORTON,** *The Parish Church c1965* W212014a

The original church was built on high ground above the River Tame, on Old Church Road. It was founded in 1347 as a chapel of ease to Aston. Water Orton became a separate parish in 1871, and the new Church of St Peter and St Paul was built of brick in 1878-79. The spire was removed in 1987 because it had become dangerously crumbly.

# INDEX

## www.francisfrith.co.uk

The Francis Frith Collection publishes over 100 new titles each year. A selection of those currently available is listed below. For latest catalogue please contact The Francis Frith Collection. **Town Books** 96 pages, approximately 75 photos. **County and Themed Books** 128 pages, approximately 135 photos (unless specified). Pocket Albums are miniature editions of Frith local history books 128 pages, approximately 95 photos.

## Available from your local bookshop or from the publisher

# The Francis Frith Collection Titles (continued)

Lancaster, Morecambe and Heysham Pocket Album
Leeds Pocket Album
Leicester
Leicestershire
Lincolnshire Living Memoires
Lincolnshire Pocket Album
Liverpool and Merseyside
London Pocket Album
Ludlow
Maidenhead
Maidstone
Malmesbury
Manchester Pocket Album
Marlborough
Matlock
Merseyside Living Memories
Nantwich and Crewe
New Forest
Newbury Living Memories
Newquay to St Ives
North Devon Living Memories
North London
North Wales
North Yorkshire
Northamptonshire
Northumberland
Northwich
Nottingham
Nottinghamshire Pocket Album
Oakham
Odiham Then and Now
Oxford Pocket Album
Oxfordshire
Padstow
Pembrokeshire
Penzance
Petersfield Then and Now
Plymouth
Poole and Sandbanks
Preston Pocket Album
Ramsgate Old and New
Reading Pocket Album
Redditch Living Memories
Redhill to Reigate
Richmond
Ringwood
Rochdale
Romford Pocket Album
Salisbury Pocket Album
Scotland
Scottish Castles
Sevenoaks and Tonbridge
Sheffield and South Yorkshire Pocket Album
Shropshire
Somerset
South Devon Coast
South Devon Living Memories
South East London
Southampton Pocket Album
Southend Pocket Album
Southport

Southwold to Aldeburgh
Stourbridge Living Memories
Stratford upon Avon
Stroud
Suffolk
Suffolk Pocket Album
Surrey Living Memories
Sussex
Sutton
Swanage and Purbeck
Swansea Pocket Album
Swindon Living Memories
Taunton
Teignmouth
Tenby and Saundersfoot
Tiverton
Torbay
Truro
Uppingham
Villages of Kent
Villages of Surrey
Villages of Sussex Pocket Album
Wakefield and the Five Towns Living Memories
Warrington
Warwick
Warwickshire Pocket Album
Wellingborough Living Memories
Wells
Welsh Castles
West Midlands Pocket Album
West Wiltshire Towns
West Yorkshire
Weston-super-Mare
Weymouth
Widnes and Runcorn
Wiltshire Churches
Wiltshire Living Memories
Wiltshire Pocket Album
Wimborne
Winchester Pocket Album
Windermere
Windsor
Wirral
Wokingham and Bracknell
Woodbridge
Worcester
Worcestershire
Worcestershire Living Memories
Wyre Forest
York Pocket Album
Yorkshire
Yorkshire Coastal Memories
Yorkshire Dales
Yorkshire Revisited

## See Frith books on the internet at www.francisfrith.com

# FRITH PRODUCTS & SERVICES

Francis Frith would doubtless be pleased to know that the pioneering publishing venture he started in 1860 still continues today. Over a hundred and forty years later, The Francis Frith Collection continues in the same innovative tradition and is now one of the foremost publishers of vintage photographs in the world. Some of the current activities include:

## Interior Decoration

Today Frith's photographs can be seen framed and as giant wall murals in thousands of pubs, restaurants, hotels, banks, retail stores and other public buildings throughout the country. In every case they enhance the unique local atmosphere of the places they depict and provide reminders of gentler days in an increasingly busy and frenetic world.

## Product Promotions

Frith products are used by many major companies to promote the sales of their own products or to reinforce their own history and heritage. Frith promotions have been used by Hovis bread, Courage beers, Scots Porage Oats, Colman's mustard, Cadbury's foods, Mellow Birds coffee, Dunhill pipe tobacco, Guinness, and Bulmer's Cider.

## Genealogy and Family History

As the interest in family history and roots grows world-wide, more and more people are turning to Frith's photographs of Great Britain for images of the towns, villages and streets where their ancestors lived; and, of course, photographs of the churches and chapels where their ancestors were christened, married and buried are an essential part of every genealogy tree and family album.

## Frith Products

All Frith photographs are available Framed or just as Mounted Prints and Posters (size 23 x 16 inches). These may be ordered from the address below. From time to time other products - Address Books, Calendars, Table Mats, etc - are available.

## The Internet

Already ninety thousand Frith photographs can be viewed and purchased on the internet through the Frith websites and a myriad of partner sites.

For more detailed information on Frith companies and products, look at these sites:

www.francisfrith.co.uk
www.francisfrith.com
*(for North American visitors)*

---

See the complete list of Frith Books at:

*www.francisfrith.co.uk*

This web site is regularly updated with the latest list of publications from The Francis Frith Collection. If you wish to buy books relating to another part of the country that your local bookshop does not stock, you may purchase on-line.

---

*For further information, trade, or author enquiries please contact us at the address below:*
**The Francis Frith Collection, Frith's Barn, Teffont, Salisbury, Wiltshire, England SP3 5QP.**
Tel: +44 (0)1722 716 376  Fax: +44 (0)1722 716 881   Email: sales@francisfrith.co.uk

# See Frith books on the internet at www.francisfrith.com

# FREE PRINT OF YOUR CHOICE

**Mounted Print**
*Overall size 14 x 11 inches (355 x 280mm)*

**Choose any Frith photograph in this book.**
Simply complete the Voucher opposite and return it with your remittance for £3.50 (to cover postage and handling) and we will print the photograph of your choice in SEPIA (size 11 x 8 inches) and supply it in a cream mount with a burgundy rule line (overall size 14 x 11 inches).
**Please note: photographs with a reference number starting with a "Z" are not Frith photographs and cannot be supplied under this offer.**
**Offer valid for delivery to one UK address only.**

*PLUS:* **Order additional Mounted Prints at HALF PRICE - £7.49 each** (normally £14.99)
If you would like to order more Frith prints from this book, possibly as gifts for friends and family, you can buy them at half price (with no additional postage and handling costs).

*PLUS:* **Have your Mounted Prints framed**
For an extra £14.95 per print you can have your mounted print(s) framed in an elegant polished wood and gilt moulding, overall size 16 x 13 inches (no additional postage and handling required).

---

**IMPORTANT!**

**These special prices are only available if you use this form to order. You must use the ORIGINAL VOUCHER on this page (no copies permitted). We can only despatch to one UK address. This offer cannot be combined with any other offer.**

---

*Send completed Voucher form to:*
**The Francis Frith Collection, Frith's Barn, Teffont, Salisbury, Wiltshire SP3 5QP**

# CHOOSE A PHOTOGRAPH FROM THIS BOOK

*Voucher* for **FREE** *and Reduced Price Frith Prints*

*Please do not photocopy this voucher. Only the original is valid, so please fill it in, cut it out and return it to us with your order.*

| Picture ref no | Page no | Qty | Mounted @ £7.49 | Framed + £14.95 | Total Cost £ |
|---|---|---|---|---|---|
| | | 1 | Free of charge* | £ | £ |
| | | | £7.49 | £ | £ |
| | | | £7.49 | £ | £ |
| | | | £7.49 | £ | £ |
| | | | £7.49 | £ | £ |
| | | | £7.49 | £ | £ |

*Please allow 28 days for delivery. Offer available to one UK address only*

| | |
|---|---|
| * Post & handling | £3.50 |
| Total Order Cost | £ |

Title of this book . . . . . . . . . . . . . . . . . . . . . . . . . . . . . . .

I enclose a cheque/postal order for £ . . . . . . . . . .
made payable to 'The Francis Frith Collection'

OR please debit my Mastercard / Visa / Maestro card, details below

Card Number

Issue No (Maestro only)          Valid from (Maestro)

Expires          Signature

Name  Mr/Mrs/Ms . . . . . . . . . . . . . . . . . . . . . . . . . . . . . . .
Address . . . . . . . . . . . . . . . . . . . . . . . . . . . . . . . . . . . . . . .
. . . . . . . . . . . . . . . . . . . . . . . . . . . . . . . . . . . . . . . . . . . . .
. . . . . . . . . . . . . . . . . . . . . . . . . . . . . . . . . . . . . . . . . . . . .
. . . . . . . . . . . . . . . . . . . . . . . . . Postcode . . . . . . . . . . . .
Daytime Tel No . . . . . . . . . . . . . . . . . . . . . . . . . . . . . . . . .
Email . . . . . . . . . . . . . . . . . . . . . . . . . . . . . . . . . . . . . . . .

ISBN 1-85937-652-5          Valid to 31/12/08

**Can you help us with information about any of the Frith photographs in this book?**

We are gradually compiling an historical record for each of the photographs in the Frith archive. It is always fascinating to find out the names of the people shown in the pictures, as well as insights into the shops, buildings and other features depicted.

If you recognize anyone in the photographs in this book, or if you have information not already included in the author's caption, do let us know. We would love to hear from you, and will try to publish it in future books or articles.

**Our production team**

Frith books are produced by a small dedicated team at offices in the converted Grade II listed 18th-century barn at Teffont near Salisbury, illustrated above. Most have worked with The Francis Frith Collection for many years. All have in common one quality: they have a passion for The Francis Frith Collection. The team is constantly expanding, but currently includes:

Andrew Alsop, Paul Baron, Jason Buck, John Buck, Jenny Coles, Heather Crisp, David Davies, Natalie Davis, Louis du Mont, Isobel Hall, Chris Hardwick, Julian Hight, Peter Horne, James Kinnear, Karen Kinnear, Tina Leary, Stuart Login, Sue Molloy, Sarah Roberts, Kate Rotondetto, Eliza Sackett, Terence Sackett, Sandra Sampson, Adrian Sanders, Sandra Sanger, Julia Skinner, Lewis Taylor, Will Tunnicliffe, David Turner and Ricky Williams.

**Free Print – see overleaf**